HOW TO RAISE TEENAGERS' SELF-ESTEEM

EN71020

by
Aminah Clark, M.A.
Harris Clemes, Ph.D.
Reynold Bean, Ed.M.

Edited by
Janet Gluckman

ENRICH
INSTRUCTIONAL
MATERIALS
DIVISION OF OHAUS® *presents* **THE WHOLE CHILD SERIES**

1980 Revised edition · Eighth Printing 1985
Copyright © 1978 Reynold Bean, Harris Clemes
Published by ENRICH, DIV./OHAUS, San Jose, CA 95131
All Rights Reserved Under International Convention
Printed in U.S.A.
ISBM 0-933358-78-4

CONTENTS

INTRODUCTION

In some primitive cultures, a formal ceremony, or "rite of passage" that lasted a few hours or a few days, marked the abrupt growing up of a child to adulthood. Adolescence was neither as difficult nor as prolonged as it is in our modern, "civilized" times.

As contemporary life has grown more complex, the period of adolescence has become a rather long, poorly defined bridge between childhood and adulthood. Certain practices show adult recognition—voting privileges, driver's licenses, graduation from high school or college, or marriage—but these turning points in an adolescent's life bring with them no guarantee of a state of readiness to assume the responsibilities that go along with them.

Anyone who deals with young people knows that the adolescent stage of development, 12 to 18 years, is critical. Parents of teenagers, and teachers who deal with teenagers don't have to be reminded of the frustration and helplessness they so often feel over the adjustments and problems adolescents run into during this time.

The child enters adolescence with many of the attitudes, feelings, skills and dependencies of his* early life, and we usually expect him to emerge from this stage fully prepared to cope as a responsible person in the adult world. In reality this preparation is often inadequate. Many young people spend part of their 20's trying to fill out the skills, self-knowledge and self-reliance they have not completed during the teen years.

Adolescence is the last stage of our children's growth in which parents and helpers can take an active role in helping set their life paths. It is the last stage in which we can be a daily example, give advice, arrange family activities, provide wide opportunities, and have direct contact with the education process. At the end of adolescence, most young people go off to work, college, marriage—in short, out into the world on their own. We must then be prepared to release them completely to have the best possible life of their own, while loving and helping them at a distance.

One of the most effective ways we can help our teenagers is to bolster their self-esteem. A strong sense of self-esteem is one of the most valuable

*He, rather than he or she, is used in the text for the sake of fluidity.

2

resources an adolescent can have. Studies have shown that the teenager with a high sense of self-esteem will learn more effectively, develop more rewarding relationships, be more able to use opportunities and work productively and be self-sufficient. He will also have a clearer sense of his own direction than the adolescent who has a low opinion of himself. Further, if the adolescent leaves this stage with a strongly developed sense of self-esteem, he may enter adulthood armed with a large part of the sound foundation he will need to lead a productive and fulfilling life.

In these times of rapid change and family disorganization, one of the most important resources you can support in your adolescent is a sense of self-worth. It is a strength he may always carry within himself and once it is strongly established, and he understands the mechanisms for keeping it healthy, he can rely on it for life.

The authors have found that it is definitely possible to enhance self-worth in young people by creating an environment where self-esteem is a valued attribute. This handbook has been prepared to help you create such an environment within your family or group. You can increase your adolescent's sense of self-esteem, and help him or her internalize principles of sound self-esteem that he or she can carry forward into adult life on a self-generating basis. And these principles are universal. You can use them to understand not only your adolescent better, but yourself and others as well.

You don't need to be a teacher or psychologist to use this handbook. After years of work with individuals of all ages, in psychological counseling, in schools, through workshops and in-service training programs, the authors have been able to develop and present a practical, step-by-step model that has already been used successfully by parents, teachers and administrators. The model, presented in this handbook, is designed to enhance understanding of adolescence and to provide clear procedures for raising teenagers' self-esteem.

— The Authors

I.
What is Self-Esteem and Why Is It Important?

Self-esteem is our sense of self-worth. It comes from all of the thoughts, feelings, sensations and experiences we have collected about ourselves through life: we think we are smart, or dumb; we feel awkward, or graceful; we like ourselves, or we don't. Thousands of impressions, evaluations and experiences we have about ourselves add up to a good feeling about our self-worth, or conversely, an uneasy feeling of inadequacy.

Everyone needs self-esteem, regardless of age, sex, cultural background, or direction and work in life. Self-esteem affects virtually every facet of life. In fact, several psychological studies indicate that unless, and until, the need for self-esteem is satisfied, the fulfillment of more expansive needs—creativity, achievement, realization of full potential—is limited. Recall how fine you felt when someone complimented your work, or you finished a project that you knew was well done. People who feel good about themselves usually feel good about life. They are able to meet and solve the challenges and responsibilities of life with confidence.

II.
The Characteristics of High and Low Self-Esteem

The teenager's sense of self-esteem will go up and down rather radically. He will express the characteristics of both high and low self-esteem described here at different times, depending somewhat on the events, people and experiences that influence him at the moment. But you will be able to observe a general underlying trend toward valuing self, or denying self, and that is the pattern you can look for over time as you consider the characteristics below:

A teenager with high self-esteem will:

- **Act independently.** *He will make choices and decisions about such issues as time usage, money, jobs, clothing, etc., and he will seek friends and entertainment on his own.*

- **Assume responsibility.** *He will act promptly and confidently, and will sometimes assume responsibility for obvious chores or needs such as dishes, yard work, comforting a friend in distress, without being asked.*

- **Be proud of accomplishments.** *He will accept acknowledgement of achievements with pleasure and even compliment himself about them now and then.*

- **Approach new challenges with enthusiasm.** *Unfamiliar jobs, new learning and activities will be interesting to him and he will involve himself confidently.*

- *Exhibit a broad range of emotions and feelings.* He will be able to laugh, giggle, shout, cry, express affection spontaneously, and in general, move through various emotions without self-consciousness.

- *Tolerate frustration well.* He will be able to meet frustration with various responses such as waiting through it, laughing at himself, speaking up firmly, etc., and can talk about what frustrates him.

- *Feel capable of influencing others.* He will be confident of his impression and effect on family members, friends and even authorities, such as teachers, ministers, bosses, etc.

A teenager with low self-esteem will:

- *Demean his own talents.* He will say, "I can't do this or that..., I don't know how..., I could never learn that."

- *Feel that others don't value him.* He will feel unsure, or downright negative, about his parents' or friends' support and affection.

- *Feel powerless.* Lack of confidence, or even helplessness will pervade many of the teenager's attitudes and actions. He will not deal forcefully with challenges or problems.

- *Be easily influenced by others.* His ideas and behavior will shift frequently, according to whom he is spending time with; he will be frequently manipulated by strong personalities.

- *Express a narrow range of emotions and feelings.* Just a few characteristic emotions, for example, nonchalance, toughness, hysteria, sulking, will be expressed repetitively. Parents can predict which stock responses can be expected for any given situation.

- *Avoid situations that provoke anxiety.* The tolerance for stress, particularly fear, anger, or chaos-provoking circumstances, will be low.

- *Become defensive and easily frustrated.* He will be "thin-skinned," unable to accept criticism or unexpected demands, and have excuses for why he couldn't perform.

- *Blame others for his own weaknesses.* He will rarely admit to mistakes or weakness and frequently name someone else, or unfortunate events, as the cause of his difficulties.

III.
How Self-Esteem Develops

The view of self and a sense of self-esteem develop gradually throughout life, beginning in infancy and progressing through stages of increasing complexity. Each stage contributes new impressions, feelings, and eventually complex thoughts about self. The sum adds up to an overall feeling of self-worth, or of inadequacy.

The infant has no "view" of himself as such. He "experiences." He has feelings and physical sensations, and a kind of vague, diffuse "awareness" based on sensations. He experiences an overall sense of well-being when he nurses, or is cuddled by parents, receives smiles, is warm and fed. He feels good when he receives basic physical needs and a warm, nourishing emotional climate. He feels uneasy or pained when his basic needs are neglected: he has to cry for a long time before being fed; he remains wet and cold; he is not protected from falling; or he has insufficient physical and emotional attention.

As the child develops, begins to learn language, experiences himself in many circumstances, and senses how others react to him, particularly mother and father, gradually he develops a sense of self. By two years of age, he has a sense of autonomy, and an awareness of himself as a separate person, rather than as an appendage of mother and father.

It is during these early stages of life that the first view of self forms. It develops almost exclusively from the reactions of others toward the child. When a parent says, "What a good girl you are," the child gains an impression of herself as being a "good girl," no matter how undefined this impression may be. She brings those words inside herself, or internalizes them. When the parents say, "You are pretty, lovable, smart, sweet," and so on, the child gradually collects these positive words inside to form a view of self, together with feelings, stimulated by smiles, cheerful and warm voices, approving nods, and physical sensations, hugs, hand-holding, stroking a hurt.

The first broad view and feeling of self is a complex impression formed from the reactions of significant others to the child. Generally, mother is the predominant figure in life at this time, if she is present. Father, other relatives and siblings also contribute to this impression to the degree that they interact with the child.

Example:

Sally was the apple of her parents' eyes. They loved their first-born daughter dearly and let her know it in many ways, by telling her, hugging her, attending to her needs. "What a wonderful girl you are," her mother would say, "so sweet and dear. Mommy loves you," with a great hug.

"How's Daddy's most favorite girl in the world today?" her father would say as he arrived from work. Both parents played with her, taught her new words, encouraged her curiosity and in general, provided a cheerful, loving environ-ment. One day, Sally was seen hugging herself, as she said: "Sally won-er-ful girl, won-er-ful girl." Sally's first impression of self was solid and positive.

This first impression will form the seed of the child's feeling of self-worth. To the extent that this view is positive, the child's feeling of himself will be strong and healthy. He will experience a sense of well-being and "o.k.-ness" that derives from acceptance, love, and positive responses of the parents. His later development will rest soundly on this foundation. But if the child experiences only negative feedback, neglect and rejection, he will automat-ically begin life with a sense of unworthiness. His thinking skills are not adequately developed to counter unfair, irrational and neurotic reactions to him. EVEN THOUGH RESPONSES OF SIGNIFICANT OTHERS MAY NOT BE BASED IN REALITY, THE CHILD WILL ACCEPT THEM AS TRUTH. Case histories of neglected and battered children show that their self-concepts are characterized by feelings of unworthiness and even a sense of evilness. "If mother hates me so much that she beats me, or yells negative things at me, there is something terrible and wrong about me," is the gist of the child's unconscious evaluation.

As the child grows and develops beyond early childhood, he enters a broader world of experience outside the family. Playmates, relatives, neigh-bors, and eventually teachers and schoolmates interact with him. Their responses add to the complex of his self-view. During this time, his perceptual and thinking skills are becoming more sophisticated and he may begin to have some capacity for evaluating a reaction to himself before simply accepting it as his own.

For example, by 4th or 5th grade a child may be able to think it over for himself when a peer says to him, "You're just dumb." He may think, "I can read as well as you; I get good grades; I know how to fix my bike," and conclude that his classmate's comment is not true. He *may* have this capacity *if* he has been taught to think for himself and *if* his view of himself is already fairly positive. But experience in schools has shown that such a capacity is not common. More often, the child internalizes such a comment and it validates negative impressions he already has about himself. Furthermore, the child with strong self-esteem may be able to reject the negative reactions of peers or "enemies," but he seldom has the strength to disqualify remarks from a person of authority—teachers, administrators or significant adults.

Example:

To demonstrate the power and endurance of others' reactions to us during these early years, let us investigate the root of Harry's low self-esteem. His view of himself as "ugly" and socially unattractive developed during the following stage: When Harry was in 5th grade, he had an argument with a girl classmate over who could play the record player first. The conflict became quite heated and at the peak of their fuss, the little girl suddenly blurted out, with great feeling, "Oh, you're nothing but a fat, ugly little boy." Unbelievable as it is to the adult mind, Harry took this comment into himself, aided by the strong emotional charge of the situation, and accepted it as truth. From that time forward, he viewed himself as ugly and unattractive to girls. Even though he developed into a very handsome young man and was seen as attractive by girls, at twenty he was still under the spell of his 5th grade classmate's assessment.

At age twenty, as a second year physics student in college, Harry thought of himself as ugly and socially unattractive. He felt awkward and out of place everywhere except the physics lab. He avoided social gatherings, but if trapped in one, he would sit in a corner, speak only when directly spoken to, and leave early. He was especially shy around girls, never dated, and even looked away when they glanced at him. Girls saw Harry as particularly handsome, but their initial attraction and advances toward him were soon thwarted by his unresponsive behavior. Although his classmates regarded Harry as attractive and intelligent, they felt uncomfortable around him. He seemed to prefer being alone. He avoided eye contact and would give the shortest possible answer to any question or attempt at striking up a conversation.

Since Harry's classmates had no idea what was in his mind, they speculated that he must feel superior to them—exactly the opposite of what he actually did feel—and was "stuck up." They soon gave up trying to be friendly with him, and thus his sense of isolation was increased.

Harry didn't think about his self-esteem, but when asked how he regarded himself, he replied: "I don't regard myself much at all, I guess."

This conscious faculty, the perception and thinking skill that allows a child to evaluate reality for himself will be one of the child's strongest defenses against unfair and irrational labels and judgments that others may impose upon him. When he meets irrationalities and injustice from others, he will suffer emotionally. But with the ability to think through a situation and its consequences, he can maintain a sense of inner strength and worthiness, and thus have a foundation for self-esteem.[1]

Adolescence is one of the most critical periods in life in terms of developing self-esteem. According to the psychoanalyst, Erik Erikson, this is the time when a person needs to gain a firm sense of IDENTITY—knowing himself as a unique individual apart from others, having a sense of his own abilities and talents, and being able to feel valuable as a person with future purpose. During these years, the child will become an adult, moving from dependence to independence and self-reliance. Many basic issues about approaching adulthood will arise, to be seriously confronted, if not completely resolved. They include choice of vocation, plans for self-support, marriage, basic philosophy of life, independence from family, and ability to relate to the opposite sex. In addition to these, unresolved conflicts from childhood will resurface and have to be handled.

Gaining identity is a large task in itself, as anyone who has had to achieve it in adulthood will testify. Gaining it during adolescence is complicated by the psycho-physical and social pressures that every teenager experiences.

This period brings powerful and confusing physical changes: bodies grow and change abruptly as the physical system prepares for full reproductive capacity. Such changes are often embarrassing for teenagers: cracking voice; gangly, awkward limbs; the onset of menstruation; developing breasts; height, either too tall or too short; stirring sexual feelings that become specific. These are only some of the many effects that a teenager can find difficult to cope with in relation to his or her peers and family. Hormonal shifts bring about unpredictable emotional states which make stability and control of emotions very difficult.

Social pressure reaches a peak as adolescent attention is drawn progressively from the family toward friends and the group. His need to belong is stronger now than at any other time of life. In order to fit in, he will often take on the characteristics and expressions in terms of dress, behavior, language, beliefs, of whatever group is open to him. Sometimes, this requires "putting down" many of the traits and life styles of his family.

The childhood view of self and sense of self-worth are brought into adolescence. During this period, they must be almost completely reworked, and many new perceptions will be added to form a more self-evaluated sense of worth.

In the "identity crisis" of adolescence, a young person will automatically question all aspects of himself, including the notions of himself he has adopted from others in the past. He may become rebellious and reject all evaluations of others, which of course demonstrates their power over him. Or, he may become so confused and unsure of himself that he will repeatedly ask others for approval and advice of all kinds. No matter how he approaches this need to gain an identity, he will undergo a critical reorganization of self-view and a resulting change in self-esteem.

Example:

At age sixteen, Dierdre was seen by her classmates and teachers as pretty and extremely bright, but unpleasant. Her recorded I.Q. was 140. She viewed herself, however, as dumb and an outsider. She deliberately wore old, shapeless clothes, let her hair hang limply over her pretty face, and refused to do anything in school except sulk. Her grades were very poor.

Dierdre's mother was a brilliant professional woman who was a perfectionist. She had great expectations for her daughter, whom she knew to be as intelligent as herself. She was furious when Dierdre abruptly stopped "performing" when she entered high school and took on a rebellious personality. The mother ranted and raved about Dierdre's poor showing in school, her lost opportunities, her ungratefulness for all the privileges she had in an outstanding family. The more she raved, the more rebellious and unsuccessful Dierdre became.

Dierdre was undergoing the crisis of identity. As a little girl, she had been able to accept, uncritically, her mother's appraisal of her abilities, and had performed to please. In adolescence, she began to question everything about her mother's ambitious personality. She saw the weaknesses and unhappiness in her family and decided these were a direct result of her mother's hard-driving professional careerism. She also decided that she would avoid these results by doing exactly the opposite from her mother. But such a rebellious approach was cutting Dierdre off from her own true nature and talents. She was stuck in confusion, not really knowing herself, but convinced that she didn't want to be like her mother.

One day, in a self-exploration fantasy in psychology class, Dierdre had a dramatic realization that moved her out of her stuck position and enabled her to explore her own nature apart from her mother and eventually discover her unique identity. In the fantasy, Dierdre traveled into her body. As she approached her heart, she saw black, murky clouds swirling all around it. She reported later that the clouds almost frightened her away from going into the heart. But she persisted, and eventually penetrated through the heart wall. There she suddenly came into a beautiful, "heavenly" place. Inside the heart, the sun was shining; there were flowering trees and singing birds. The air was sweet and clear. Dierdre sat down in this place in her fantasy and allowed herself to feel the peace, promise and nourishment of it for a long time. Dierdre got the message of her fantasy immediately. She realized that black, murky clouds of confusion were surrounding and blocking her true self, but that beneath them lay the beautiful, expansive and valuable core of her own being. From that day forward, Dierdre began to honor and investigate her own unique worth. Her behavior changed from non-productive to creative. She was on her way to gaining her own identity.

Ideally, the adolescent's view of self should result from this extensive re-evaluation of self. It should be based on information the adolescent himself has assessed and integrated, if identity is to be gained and self-esteem furthered. Such a view can provide the foundation of self-esteem for the rest of life. In adulthood, it will be continually updated during healthy growth, but if the foundation is weak, that growth will be greatly impaired.

IV.
How Self-Esteem
Affects Daily Life

A sense of self-esteem affects how an adolescent:

- *feels about himself*
- *thinks, learns and creates*
- *evaluates himself*
- *relates to others*
- *behaves*

The way an adolescent views himself is related to every thought, feeling and action that comes from him. When he views himself positively, he enjoys high self-esteem, whereas a negative view of self is associated with low self-esteem.

A person with high self-esteem will express his good feelings about himself and others in many subtle ways: he smiles, returns eye contact, stands straight, extends his hand in greeting, and in general, puts out a positive "feeling." Others respond to that positive feeling in like ways: they accept, and are attracted to him, they feel comfortable in his presence and thus feel good about themselves as well. Conversely, a person with low self-esteem, like Harry, puts out his own feelings of inadequacy toward others as a kind of vague distress signal. We can interpret that signal as something wrong with Harry, or with ourselves. In either case, our response is similar; we tend to shy away.

Behavior is greatly affected by self-esteem. We tend to behave according to how we view ourselves and our sense of self-esteem. And the behavior, in turn, usually validates the self view we already have. A cyclical process keeps reinforcing our basic views and attitudes.

Example:

Rick had been told many times that he was a brat, disruptive and disagreeable. He thought of himself as the kid who always caused trouble. He spent a lot of time thinking about ways he could cause trouble; after all, that was his distinction. He teased his sister incessantly; he hid the neighbor kid's bike; he poured plaster-of-paris in the art room sink. Each of these acts, and many like them, brought Rick the desired result—he preserved his self-image as the "bratty, trouble-causer." And Rick was so desperate for attention that he was also willing to take the inevitable painful consequences. (See figure 1.)

Several common motives guide behavior. These motives may conflict with each other, resulting in stress for an individual and those around him. An adolescent will tend to:

1. act in ways that confirm his self-image.

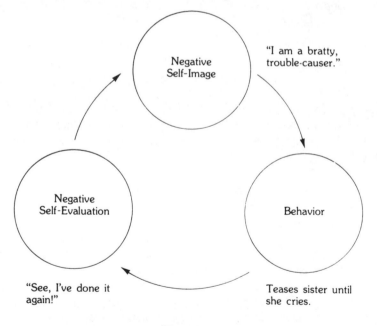

Figure 1

2. behave so as to increase his sense of worth.

3. act so as to maintain a consistent self-image, irrespective of changing circumstances.

If these motives are in conflict with each other, the teenager will seem to act erratically or irrationally. He many continue to repeat some act that gets disapproval or punishment, over and over again. When asked why he does it, he will say, "I don't know."

When self-image is positive and self-esteem high, teenagers feel capable and think confidently, thus tending to behave in successful ways which further increase their sense of self-worth:

Example:

Judy viewed herself as pretty, intelligent, popular and capable. When there was a job to be done, she attacked it with enthusiasm, confident in her abilities. Because of her capabilities and dependability, she was often asked to participate in school activities and projects which increased her opportunities to learn, expand her abilities, and her experience of success. (See figure 2.)

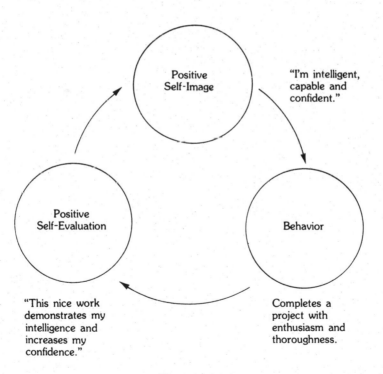

Figure 2

On the other hand, with a negative self-image and low self-esteem, people feel inadequate, think of themselves as being unable to perform and thus often block opportunities to behave successfully:

Example:

Naomi thought of herself as unattractive and had little confidence in her ability to do anything "right." She never volunteered for special projects or activities, afraid that she couldn't contribute as much as others did. She stuck to the few things she felt secure in handling—baby sitting, math lessons and playing checkers. Many of her inherent talents went unexposed and undeveloped since she could not risk the embarrassment of failure, and an even worse self-image. Since she had little practice in trying new activities, she was awkward and timid with unfamiliar tasks and settings. She came across as a weak contributor and thus felt unsuccessful. (See figure 3.)

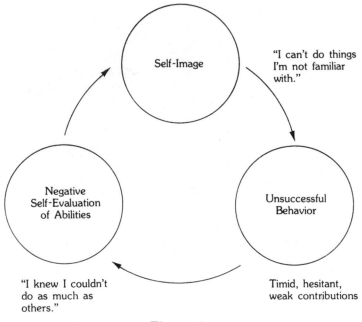

Figure 3

Self-esteem affects learning. Research about self-image and academic performance shows a strong reciprocal relationship between self-esteem and the ability to learn.[2] High self-esteem promotes learning. The teenager who enjoys high self-esteem learns more happily and easily than one who feels inadequate about himself; he will tackle new learning tasks with confidence and enthusiasm. His performance will tend to be successful, since thought and feeling precede action, and he is already "set" with positive expectations. Successful performance then reinforces his good feelings; he will view himself as being more competent with each successful achievement.

Example:

When Judy, (introduced on page 21), was a junior in high school, she was asked to help formulate a "Big Sister" program for incoming freshmen. The project required sensitivity to the problems and feelings of 13-year olds, the ability to think through and organize workable procedures, and the willingness to work agreeably with others, both teenagers and adults. These are mature qualities that are not always demonstrated, even by adults. But administration and faculty believed they could rely on Judy to do a good job because of her demonstrated competence in other projects and her warm and cheerful manner towards others. She accepted the challenge, learned a great deal about organization, leadership and problems of other students, and helped bring about a successful program. (See figure 4.)

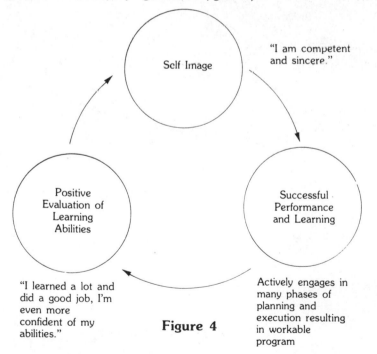

Figure 4

23

But the person who believes that he is inadequate and unable to learn will approach each new learning task with a sense of hopelessness and dread. "Failure syndrome" is a well known phenomenon in education: the child who has had early failures in school will develop attitudes of "I can't do it..., no use for me to try again." Consequently, he will almost inevitably fail at whatever task he halfheartedly tries, unless and until the cycle can be broken with a renewed sense of his own worth and power.

Example:

John had a difficult start in school; his family moved three times during his first year. At the end of first grade, his classmates were easily reading beginning books, but John couldn't read at all. In second grade, he was naturally put in the "low" reading group. He began to feel inadequate and helpless as a reader as he watched the other groups move along swiftly through book after book. When it was his turn to read, he became very anxious, afraid to expose his inability to recognize words in front of his classmates. Reading period became an unpleasant, embarrassing time for John. Anxiety alone prevented him from listening, thinking or seeing well; he made up excuses for avoiding it as much as possible, and thus dropped further and further behind. By his third year in school, John thought of himself as a "bad reader" and had little hope of ever catching up with his class; he felt too defeated to really try the various special techniques his teacher proposed to improve his reading skill. (See figure 5.)

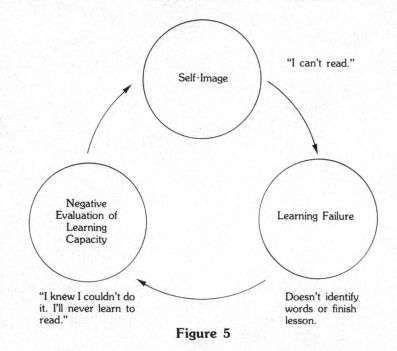

Figure 5

24

Self-esteem affects relationships and is affected by them. Cooper-smith has noted that children with high self-esteem usually have better interpersonal relationships and are often chosen for leadership positions.[3] Such children gain a feeling of acceptance from others and have a sense of influence in their relationships.

The person who feels good about himself will not be excessively dependent on others for recognition, motivation, or direction. Thus he is in a better position to cooperate in the give and take of healthy relationships. He will be able to accept what others can give, without needing to "hang on" to them for self-validation.

Adolescence is a period in which the need to share and group with peers reaches a peak. To some extent, the teenager will form his view of self and the sense of self-esteem from reactions of peers to him. If he has many friends and a sense of belonging to peer groups, his feelings of self-worth will increase. But if he is isolated and ineffective in relationships during this period, he will tend to evaluate himself negatively. The teenager needs to receive acceptance and respect in relationships. Only to the extent that he has received them in the family and school before this period, will he be able to show similar respect and acceptance towards others.

Self-esteem affects creativity. Creative expression requires risk-taking and organization of resources in a unique manner. Self-assurance and a feeling of competence enables one to take risks. The adolescent who has high self-esteem will usually demonstrate creativity in much that he does. He will receive approval then for unique and outstanding productivity which further enhances his high self-esteem. Adolescents with low self-esteem fear to make mistakes that result in disapproval; they tend to be overly cautious and avoid experimental and creative expression.

How we view ourselves and the strength of our self-esteem affects every facet of our lives; it affects how we think, feel and act. In turn, almost everything we do, or don't do, influences our feelings and view of self. Self-esteem waxes and wanes throughout life. How we feel about ourselves is dependent on the way that we respond to circumstances which are unpredicted or beyond our control. A feeling of self-worth grows as we accumulate more experiences which we use as reference points for new experiences; as we become more adept at controlling the kind of experiences which we have; and as we become more skillful at containing our fears and anxieties. Some adolescents who *appear* to have high self-esteem depend on a narrowness of experience to support their feelings of self-confidence.

V.
The Benefits of
High Self-Esteem
to the Adolescent

The benefits of high self-esteem to the adolescent are many. Most importantly, the adolescent who has high self-esteem will have a greater opportunity to realize his IDENTITY during this appropriate time, when he is preparing for adulthood and before he must assume full responsibility for his life.

Other effects that will strengthen his abilities for adult life are:

- clarity of self-strengths, resources, interests and directions, i.e.

  The person who knows and respects his personal resources will attract and seize opportunities to use them.

- effectiveness and satisfaction in interpersonal relationships, i.e.

  The adolescent who learns how to relate effectively to others will have a strong ability to fulfill his social and personal needs throughout life.

- clarity of direction, i.e.

  When he has self confidence, the adolescent is better able to analyze and choose appropriate directions for adult life.

- personal productivity—at home, in school, and at work in later life, i.e.

  The adolescent who feels competent and valuable will want to perform and learn how to use his time effectively.

By helping adolescents enhance their self-esteem, you can promote these benefits and greatly strengthen their resources for adult life. The adolescent has a real need to realize his identity and feel good about himself. If he can gain satisfaction of this need at the appropriate time, ideally before he is twenty, he will carry it forward and be ready to assume responsibility for fulfilling his own needs of adulthood. But when self-esteem is not adequate, the teenager will continue to spend his energies seeking ways to feel worthwhile in all that he does.

VI.
The Four Conditions of Self-Esteem

Self-esteem develops when the primary needs of life have been appropriately satisfied. The authors have found that high self-esteem can be gained when children and teenagers experience positive feelings within four distinct conditions. They are:

CONNECTIVENESS: the feeling a teenager has when he can gain satisfaction from associations that are significant to him, and these associations are affirmed by others.

UNIQUENESS: the special sense of self a teenager feels when he can acknowledge and respect qualities or attributes that make him special and different, and when he receives respect and approval from others for these qualities.

POWER: a sense that comes from having the resources, opportunity and capability to influence the circumstances of their lives in important ways.

MODELS: reference points that provide the teenager with human, philosophical, and operational examples that help him establish meaningful values, goals, ideals and personal standards.

All four of these conditions should be present continuously for a high sense of self-esteem to be developed and maintained. No one condition is more important than another. If any one condition is not adequately provided for, there is a decrease or distortion of self-esteem.

Parents can influence the teenager's self-esteem by organizing new experiences, and relating in appropriate ways within these conditions. The remainder of this manual is about the four conditions, how problems arise within them, and what you can do to improve the climate and workability of each. You will find out how to observe your teenagers' attitudes and behavior within each of the conditions. And you will learn how to evaluate which conditions need to be changed or expanded to more adequately fulfill your adolescent's needs.

VII.
Connectiveness

A teenager will have a firm sense of Connectiveness when he has experienced "being connected" to:

- his own body and awareness, sensitivity and resources

- important persons: parents, friends, siblings, relatives, teachers

- people in important roles or positions: doctors, teachers, co-workers, ministers

- groups of common interest, purpose or heritage: cultural, social, sports, ethnic

- institutions: church, school, state, country

- objects, places or activities: place of birth, home, secret places, favorite shirt or dress, pets, sports, car, hobbies, important events

Connectiveness in Adolescence

The adolescent will experience many dramatic shifts in his connections to family, friends and the world around him. He will be breaking connections with childhood and exploring new connections with adulthood, and will progressively move away from a dependent relationship to family, toward ultimate independence. In the light of his growing awareness, and the necessity of finding himself in his own way, a teenager's re-evaluation of his parents may go hard for the once-idealized mother and father. He will compare them with other adults. He will inevitably find out about some of his parents' weaknesses and mistakes, and this knowledge may make him insecure and angry. He may lash out at them and reject their ideas, standards and life style out-of-hand. These, and other more gentle disconnecting behaviors, are a necessary part of separating himself from parents and finding his own identity.

Childhood connections *must* be broken or changed, but this process is often disruptive for both teenagers and parents. After years of being responsible for nurturing, protecting and guiding a child, the parent often finds it hard to simply cut loose thoughts *for* his teenager about safety, right decisions, consequences of actions, etc. Can we really trust our teenagers to know enough and to possess the strength of character and purpose to make a productive and happy way for themselves? If you, as a parent, cannot find this trust for your teenager, you will suffer prolonged anxiety and guilt within yourself and obstruct the separation process of your adolescent. If you haven't been preparing throughout your child's life to let go at the appropriate time, you will need to face the issue squarely now, during adolescence. You can review the values, discipline and opportunities you have already provided in your child's life and hope they will have become a guiding part of him.

The values you have already taught and exemplified—honesty, self-respect, commitment to responsibilities, caring for others, and the like—may not be expressed as clearly as you would like by your adolescent during this transition stage. But if you have attended to them early in his life, the chances are solid that they will become guiding principles in his adult life, after the chaos and confusion of separation have settled. Even if you are insecure about your preparation of the child, it is time now to make way for a new adult-to-adult relationship. Though you can still influence and gently guide him by having an adult-to-adult interaction, he will no longer accept, rightfully, the continuation of a parent-to-child connection with you. You must give over more and more responsibility for his own choices and behavior to your teenager.

Connectiveness with peers will change in character, from play-oriented ties to rehearsal of adult relationships. Affections and attractions toward the opposite sex become very important and sexual feelings naturally develop. The countless hours that adolescents spend talking to one another, in person and on the phone, often drive parents crazy, but this is one way they are defining themselves, by hearing themselves talk and getting responses from peers.

Example:

Barbara had been the "perfect" daughter for her parents. She was beautiful, creatively talented, and had always performed successfully in school. John was in Barbara's class, but she had never known him at all; he had been seriously crippled by a childhood disease, was undersized for his age, and was rarely able to participate in the usual social or athletic activities. He was extremely intelligent, but did not perform well in school. He was a loner who felt cut off from his peers, since the physical problems he dealt with were so different from theirs.

Barbara and John started working together in a drama class when each revealed a particularly sensitive theatrical talent. They got the lead parts in the senior play which was a demanding piece about an intimate adolescent relationship. Throughout many weeks of working on their roles together and rehearsals with the whole cast, John and Barbara got to know each other in a completely new way. Barbara quickly recognized John's basic intelligence and sensitivity and appreciated him. When John experienced the admiration of Barbara, the prettiest and most popular girl in the class, and his drama teacher and the other players, he began to get a new view of himself and his ability to relate to his peers. John's and Barbara's creative talents stimulated each other; a beautiful flowering began to happen in both. The play was an impressive success. School and community praised it. Barbara and John were stars; she had realized yet another talent within herself and he had gained a new acceptance and appreciation from peers, and decided to run for a class office. A new sense of Connectiveness had developed in both.

But marked changes in Barbara brought about a break in connectiveness with parents. She concentrated so completely on the play preparation that her academic studies were neglected; grades fell. She began to think of new life directions, and in fact, to think in many new ways as a result of her long hours with John and the play cast. When her parents wanted her to stop spending so much time on the play, she began to tell little lies about where she was going, and with whom. Her parents were shocked and disapproving of the relationship they felt was developing between the two young people. Frightened and confused, they set restrictions on all her activities and threatened to force her to leave the play altogether. As her parents became more controlling and suspicious, Barbara, for the first time, became rebellious. She saw her parents as wanting her to perform only in the ways that would bring credit to them, and not ways compatible with her own talents and interests. The parents, on the other hand, were completely at a loss to understand how their "perfect" daughter had suddenly become non-communicative, deceitful and irresponsible. A tremendous communication gap developed between them.

Developing a Sense of Connectiveness: Problems and Solutions

When teenagers lack a fulfilling sense of Connectiveness, it will show in the way they relate to individuals, groups and things. If you will "step back" in your view of a young person for a few days and observe him objectively, you will be able to evaluate whether he has a firm sense of Connectiveness, or whether he has a problem in that condition and needs your assistance.

PROBLEMS WITH CONNECTIVENESS

A teenager who cannot gain adequate satisfaction from connections in his life will probably act in one or several of the ways described below. Naturally, most people will act in some of these ways, some of the time. But you can be fairly sure that your teenager has a problem with Connectiveness if: i) you find a *pattern* of one of these behaviors in his life, that is, he repeats a particular mood or action over and over, ii) *intense feelings* arise with one or several of these behaviors, especially anger or despondency, or iii) *several indicators* show up on a continuing basis.

Problems with Connectiveness can be observed in some of the following behaviors, i.e. if a teenager:

- does not communicate easily and is unable to listen to others and understand their point of view
- is shy, has few or no friends, and actively avoids social situations; is unaware of others' interests or needs
- talks negatively about family, race or ethnic group
- seldom, if ever, volunteers to help others
- is disliked by peers
- acts uncomfortable around adults, or else constantly seeks their attention
- always wants to be in the center of things and/or constantly tries to get others to notice him
- more often relates to things or animals than people; carries lots of "stuff" around in pockets, bags, etc., and values it excessively; spends a lot of time with pets, takes them to bed, etc.
- has trouble stating his ideas or feelings directly and asking for what he needs.
- is uncomfortable in touching others, or being touched

If you observe your teenager acting in several of these ways, or in one of them constantly, you will know that his sense of Connectiveness can be improved.

RELATING TO THE TEENAGER
WHO HAS A LOW SENSE OF CONNECTIVENESS

There are a number of things you can do to help the teenager with a low sense of Connectiveness. They will require opening your awareness to new perspectives and in some cases breaking old habit patterns. But if you will *do* some of these things, even if they feel awkward at first, you will notice a change in your teenager's response to you and others. That change will be very subtle at first (teenagers have a certain stubbornness about giving up their favorite, and secure, relations), or you may not see any change at all in the first few tries. But if you will persist, you will find the new action becoming easier each time you do it, and you will soon notice progressively positive responses. And a teenager can change faster than an adult. He is open to new ways of relating, particularly when they bring increased personal satisfaction.

Give personal attention to a teenager when he needs it. You will have to notice this need from his behavior. He will hang around, ask questions, be moody; he will not usually ask directly. Listen to him carefully, look at him directly, and let him know by your response that you have understood what he is saying. Listen non-judgmentally. It's not necessary to comment on everything he says or to correct him all the time, but let him know you have heard. Undistracted attention is *quality* attention; a small amount of it will be more valuable than lots of half-hearted recognition.

Show affection in what you say and do. Simple declarations of affection—"I love you..., I like you a lot..., You're o.k."—may elicit a momentary scoff, but the teenager is inwardly pleased and nourished by them. Smile, let warmth come through your tone of voice, wink to show recognition. Touch and hug when it is appropriate. Some teenagers are uncomfortable when parents hug or kiss them, but they still appreciate a pat on the shoulder or a gentle nudge.

Be specific with praise. Tell a teenager *what* he did, or *how* he acted, that you like. Say, "I really appreciate the way you cleaned the table." "How beautifully you finished the macrame." Make sure he sees, hears or feels your approval, not just your criticism for mistakes or misbehavior. Encourage him to praise himself for jobs well done.

Show approval when a teenager relates well to others. Praise considerate behavior; make a special point of it when you see him cooperating and being helpful to others as well as you. Also encourage him to take credit, and praise himself, for successful interaction with others.

Respect your teenager's relationships with friends by providing opportunities for them to visit in your home and by showing your acceptance. Take an interest in friends when possible and allow your home to be a welcoming, comfortable and attractive place for them. It is embarrassing to teenagers and limits friendships when there are conditions at home, physical or psychological, which they don't want friends to view.

Share your own feelings with teenagers. Let them know how things affect you. Say, "I feel good when we can speak honestly to one another...;" "I'm sad about what happened yesterday...;" "I get really irritated when you break an agreement." Make it clear what you like and don't like. Admitting your feelings isn't a sign of weakness and doesn't jeopardize your role as parent or guide, but rather helps you move toward the adult-to-adult relationship you need to establish.

Share your interests, hobbies, and some of your life concerns with the adolescent. Obviously it isn't appropriate to burden him with serious adult problems, but it is a time when you can share more complicated interests and activities with him than you could during his childhood.

Occasionally do something special for a teenager that satisfies his particular needs or interests. Take him to a laboratory, or museum, where he can find out more about a specific interest he has. Take him shopping by himself for a special outfit. Give a party for his choral or drama group.

Spend time alone with the teenager, when needs of other family members are not a distraction. Plan a camping trip, even an afternoon at a movie, or athletic event. Several hours without disruption give the teenager, who may be struggling with many issues internally, the time to unwind, test your receptiveness, and finally come out with a problem or concern that he needs help with. The parent who takes a teenager into a room, closes the door and says, "Now, let's talk about sex," is not apt to get anywhere.

If your teenager is particularly shy, you will need to be content with very little or no response when you talk with him. He may be unable to express his feelings at the time, but usually he will show in later behavior that he got your point.

IMPROVING YOUR FAMILY'S SENSE OF CONNECTIVENESS

Every family or group has a particular "climate" that has developed from the feelings, attitudes, ways of communicating and rules that have infused family members' time together. A young person's sense of Connectiveness will have a great deal to do with the quality of interpersonal relationships within his family.

Activities and attitudes that go on among family members reflect the level of Connectiveness in the family, and also set a pattern for their relationships outside the family. When interactions are predominantly positive, characterized by respect, acceptance and caring among family members, the sense of Connectiveness is high. In contrast, negative feelings and habit patterns, such as arguing, lack of respect for others' opinions, time or possessions, promote a climate of separateness where each member is on his own to sink or swim.

A sense of Connectiveness among all family or group members can be built when positive interactions are encouraged between them. The following ideas can help you promote a positive climate for family relationships and enhance each member's sense of Connectiveness. But before you begin a program for positive change within your family, it would be good to talk it over among yourselves, at least between parents, and when possible, with all family members, to assess which new habits can most appropriately be started in your situation. The more acceptance and enthusiasm you can enlist from family members at the beginning, the better your chances for success. And DON'T EXPECT GREAT CHANGES OVERNIGHT. Revising or reversing old negative habits and initiating new ways of relating will take time. You can't expect everyone to get the message and cooperate immediately, especially if you have had a negative climate within your family. Teenagers may not know how to handle new kinds of relationships. They may not feel sure they can trust you to keep a new program going. You will need to provide a wide acceptance level, and time for mistakes, falling back into old habits, and simply learning the style of new ones. Give everyone, including yourself, time to learn and adjust. If you have patience and diligence in the beginning, you will begin to experience rewarding change within a few months.

Create opportunities for family members to work and play together. Plan family trips, picnics, holiday celebrations, even watching a particular TV program together. Having fun together shakes out some of the tensions and misunderstandings that have grown between us and allows new connections and appreciations to develop. Events should be planned on a fairly regular basis and in such a way that interests of all the family members can be included. Create projects that can involve the whole family in cooperative tasks toward a common goal. Give teenagers a say in the planning and execution of them. Painting a mural, or part of the house, building a barbeque or redecorating the family room, and other such activities can be planned so that each member contributes and gains pride in a common effort.

Set aside regular times for family sharing. Plan a "family night" once a week, or even twice monthly—consistency is more important than frequency. A special dinner or refreshments marks a special time together and can provide an opportunity to share personal experiences, discuss family issues and problems, set project goals or plan activities for the future. This is also an excellent time for sharing special talents of family members—John may sing a new song he's written; Sally can present a scene from a play she's doing at school; Tim might play his guitar. One family member each time can be given the responsibility for planning and coordinating the event.

Arrange daily life so that the whole family is together at least once a day. Dinnertime is often the most logical time for everyone to touch in. It is important to keep the continuity of family life active. Current concerns of family members, as well as broader community, national and international issues can be discussed at such a time. Encourage teenagers to voice their opinons and share your own. Keep this time for positive interaction. See that everyone can participate. Save passive or singular activities such as reading the newspaper, watching TV, or dealing with necessary negative issues, (marital arguments, criticism), for other times.

Encourage participation in cultural programs and community services. Participate with your family in community service projects, such as environmental clean-ups, services to senior citizens and the like. Take all or some members of the family to lectures, concerts and museums. Such activities not only promote family cohesion, but they broaden teenagers' aesthetic values.

Support teenagers' school and community efforts by attending programs and performances. Encourage their participation in school activities and attend the big events—sports matches, drama productions, award nights—yourself. Unlike the younger child who begs Mom and Dad to attend every single program, the teenager is often embarrassed to ask parents to come to "back-to-school" night, or to see him play in the game, or a school drama. You will have to keep track of such programs through school bulletins or off-hand remarks. He will always secretly appreciate your support. It's very important for him to see Mom and/or Dad in the audience, but he probably won't ask, or thank you.

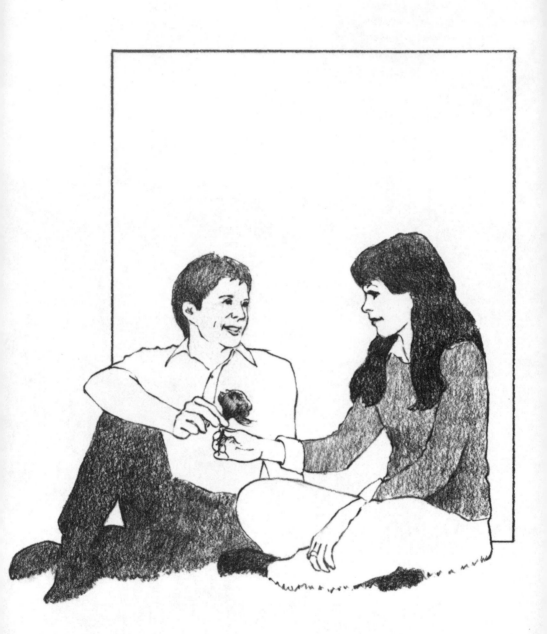

VIII.
Uniqueness

A teenager with a healthy sense of Uniqueness acknowledges and respects his own special qualitites or attributes, and receives affirmation from others that those qualities are valuable. Such attributes must be experienced as special by the adolescent who needs to:

- feel that he knows, or can do, things that no one else knows or can do
- be aware that others think he has special qualities
- respect himself as an individual
- know he is imaginative or creative
- enjoy the feeling of being different, without having to make others uncomfortable

What adults perceive as unique about their teenager may not seem so to him.

As a teenager receives affirmation from others that his qualities are special, his self-esteem will be raised. When he suffers criticism, punishment or shame from others about those qualities, his self-esteem will be lowered.

Uniqueness can be felt by a person about any one, or a combination of, the following things:

body qualities	*favorite activities*
appearance	*roles or functions*
special skills	*imagination*
talents	*knowledge*
social or cultural background	*world-view*
vocational interests	*hobbies*

Uniqueness in Adolescence

The first real sense of self develops in early childhood, (2–3 years), when a child gains a feeling of being somebody apart from parents. During that time, he exerts strong will to express himself. In adolescence, this separate sense of self re-emerges. Everyone has a "true self," a unique core that distinguishes him from all others and which the great psychologist, Carl Jung, called the "Self." This Self holds wisdom and direction for the individual. A person who is in touch with it will know the talents, strengths and inclinations that are special to him. He will also have a feeling of the right directions for him to complete life tasks. Some people spend years in self-exploration to gain a strong contact with this Self, while others seem to have it automatically.

The adolescent can be very close to this Self. He is in a period of awakening; often his hunches, feelings and dreams come from his own inner wisdom. Biographies of great leaders, explorers and inventors frequently describe insights or visions during thier teen years which set up a lifetime direction. Many American Indian tribes had a particular ritual for the adolescent to induce his own "vision;" it was accepted that the resulting dream or vision gave the young person his vocation and direction in life.

Before he enters into the outer-directed responsibilities of adulthood, the adolescent has a particular opportunity to explore his unique self. He is not yet distracted by the prime responsibility for his own survival; he can dream, play around with ideas, talents and creative possibilites. The young person who says, "I need to find myself," as he explores various questionable activities, friendships and talents, may annoy his parents who are preoccupied with the hard realities of providing a livelihood. They may fear some of the "kooky" ideas, dress or activities that seem to consume their children. They are embarrassed when their teenager seems strange—an "oddball." Yet diverse explorations are necessary during this period for the adolescent. His drive to "find himself" is truly based on an inner necessity. Parents who understand this need, who may even assist it, will one day see these sometimes erratic and peculiar seeds of uniqueness blossom into true individuality as their son or daughter matures. Putting up with some craziness now can allow the completion of a whole human being later on.

Example:

Brent was a particularly nondescript boy. He was small for his age, soft-spoken, artistic and a "sissy," according to other boys. He had never shown any noteworthy successes or talents in school, but his mother regarded him as a very special person.

When he was fifteen, Brent began to investigate subjects that interested him—psychology, philosophy, ancient history. He was fascinated by anything about ancient Egypt and began to make extraordinary drawings and paintings in an ancient Egyptian style. His mother was interested in, and encouraged, his extra-curricular studies, and talked with him about them.

During this time, Brent began to have a series of long and complicated dreams which seemed to contain messages or instructions for him. He was at first confused and frightened by the dreams, but he sought out the psychology teacher to describe and discuss them. She listened attentively and encouraged him to keep a journal of the dreams. A definite pattern was discovered in the dreams, and they did give instructions for particular studies Brent should pursue. Supported by his mother and the psychology teacher, Brent continued to read and think about "esoteric" questions which would ordinarily have been considered too mature for him. He enrolled in the psychology class. His grasp of psychological and philosophical concepts made his classmates suspicious. They thought he must be putting on an act.

Brent was not intimidated by his peers and continued to study deeply and widely and to discuss his ideas with the psychology teacher and his ever-supportive mother, who regarded him as her intellectual equal. Through group work and co-counseling in his psychology class, Brent demonstrated wisdom, compassion and intelligence to his peers. Gradually, they experienced that his grasp of the subject was not a pretense, and they began to turn to him for insight and advice. By the end of the year, Brent had become something of a father figure in the class, and his uniqueness was gratefully accepted.

Brent's personal uniqueness, the talents he had uncovered, and the interests and knowledge he had gained during this time, expanded during subsequent years. His dreams had given valid direction for him, and fortunately he had received enough support of his unique Self at a crucial time to be able to follow them.

Brent is a true, if very unusual, person. His mother was also unusual, in that she was able to accept and encourage Brent's uniqueness at an early age. The inherent potential of our young people might be released much earlier if we were able to accept and respect their uniqueness.

Developing a Sense of Uniqueness: Problems and Solutions

A sense of Uniqueness will develop when the special qualities and unusual characteristics of individuals are accepted and encouraged within your family. You can help raise your teenager's self-esteem by relating to him in ways that honor his individuality.

PROBLEMS WITH UNIQUENESS

As you observe a teenager's behavior, remember that you are watching for repetition of a pattern, intense feelings, or several of these indicators expressed on a continuing basis. The teenager with a low sense of Uniqueness will behave in one or several of the following ways:

- speak negatively about himself and his accomplishments

- take little or no pride in his appearance

- show little imagination and rarely come up with original ideas

- demonstrate little regard for his own ideas, interests, or abilities. He will rarely express an opinion or feeling that is different from others.

- do things the way he is told, rarely improvising from his own awareness

- be uncomfortable when called on or singled out

- seek praise or recognition often, but become embarrassed, deny or disregard it when it is given

- show off when it is inappropriate

- usually conform to others', particularly peers', wishes and ideas. He follows, and rarely leads.

- interact with others in a stilted, mechanical way, rather than spontaneously or creatively. He will tend to categorize others in a simplistic way, and perhaps be critical of their personal characteristics. He will try to find the ways he is like others, rather than accept differences.

RELATING TO THE TEENAGER WHO HAS A LOW SENSE OF UNIQUENESS

If your teenager shows through his behavior that his sense of Uniqueness is low, you can help by relating to him in some of the following ways:

Notice and affirm his special characteristics and talents. Observe your teenager carefully, setting aside for a while your own wishes and beliefs about him. Find out what his distinct talents and strengths are. When you have located them, give them power by affirming them. Affirmation is the act of strongly confirming that something exists, or is true. When we affirm some quality or act of a teenager, we give it power, imprinting it into his mind and behavior for the future. Affirming another person lets him know he is significant or important. Such positive affirmations as: "You did a beautiful job on this essay...; You have such a lovely smile...; I appreciate your honesty," encourage the behavior they compliment. Negative attention to a quality or act, through such statements as: "You never finish a job properly...; Can't you ever say something nice?; You're always late anyway," tend to encourage repetition of the very qualities we are criticizing. By affirming your teenager's positive qualities, you can encourage them *and* raise his self-esteem.

Accept and encourage your teenager to express his own ideas, even when they are different from your own. He will necessarily be fooling around with a lot of "half-baked" notions, plans and visions, at least compared to your developed thinking. This is the way he tries out his own thinking processes. Even if you can't agree with him—and many times you won't—let him know you respect his thinking ability.

Communicate acceptance of the teenager, even when his behavior must be limited. You can love and respect a teenager even if you don't like what he's doing right now, if you understand and accept him. Let him know that your love and support for him as a person are constant while you are setting limits. Say: "I can *understand* what you did, but it wasn't appropriate in that situation."

Find the positive aspects of unusual ideas or behavior and compliment them. Let your teenager know it's o.k. to be different. You may wish to describe some of your own unique qualities which have subsequently become an important part of your life, but were misunderstood, or not supported, in adolescence.

Accept a teenager's necessary experimentation with jobs, activities and philosophies. He may try several part-time jobs, go through numerous activity fads or adopt different "causes" in rapid succession. Such experimentation is not a sign of instability or irresponsibility at this age. It is often necessary exploration of the world; a trial and error process for fitting talents with opportunities.

Respect adolescent visions. Idealistic plans for the future, and utopian schemes of the teenager may seem completely unrealistic to adults who have often shelved their own youthful dreams under the impact of survival realities. But visions and dreams provide the inspiration for change and growth, inventions and discoveries. Talk over their hopes and visions with your teenagers. You may gently point out some of the realities of execution, but let them take the lead in their own paths. Ask yourself whether you subtly attempt to "put your own trip" on your teenager, expecting him to fulfill the hopes and dreams you didn't, or whether you are really able to honor his unique individuality and encourage him to enter adult life to fulfill his own potential, within his own work.

Respect the uniqueness and privacy of the teenager's room and possessions. He may decorate his room in ways that seem ugly or bizarre to you, but these expressions are important to his investigation of his own tastes and methods. His possessions may seem sentimental, peculiar or worthless to you, but each sacred relic—prom programs, beach rocks, dried flowers, bug specimens—is an expression of a unique interest or moment to him.

Allow the teenager to perform his responsibilities in his own way so that he can gain operational knowledge of his special qualities and talents. He may fix the car or clean the house according to a formula very different from yours, but this is the way he discovers himself.

IMPROVING YOUR FAMILY'S SENSE OF UNIQUENESS

Each member of your family can enjoy a sense of Uniqueness when there is a wide acceptance level in the family for individual differences, and those differences are valued for their enrichment of the whole group.

Consider personal needs of each member of the family when you are planning activities, setting policies or determining goals. It is not always possible to integrate the needs of each family member into a family plan. But being aware of, and discussing the individual needs and interests of all members, will show your respect for their separate concerns. For example, when you are planning a family summer vacation, you will need to consult the plans and schedules of your teenagers far in advance, so that a time can be found when they can join the family without having to give up some valued plan, such as summer school, music camp, or trips with friends.

Encourage individual growth of family members by accepting their various investigations of new ideas, interests, vocational directions, philosophies, or religions. You might historically be a family of scholars, or farmers, or readers, or ball players, but sons and daughters need the freedom to explore their own directions, and sample values or philosophies that are different from those of their parents.

Promote social growth by accepting new relationships and familiarity with diverse organizations and activities. Young people broaden their understanding and practice social skills when they interact with people outside their family groups. Families with different life styles from your own, clubs that undertake group trips or social service projects, elaborate social events, such as proms, weddings, etc.—all these give training in appropriate manners and interpersonal skills.

Ask teenagers to contribute their special talents or interests to your family life. Give them tasks that will engage their special qualities. Provide opportunities for creative expression in the family. Talk to teenagers about their particular strengths and special role in your family. Each person can make a particular contribution, kindness, honesty, creativity, mechanical ability, etc., to the family that will help all other members when special qualities are recognized and valued.

Whenever possible, use democratic practices when planning policies and procedures for your family. Make it a practice to ask teenagers to voice their own needs and ideas when you are deciding family rules and procedures. Don't require that *your* rules be slavishly followed, but arrive at policies that make sense for everyone, through majority vote or concensus. Ask teenagers' ideas about implementation of the rules, and consequences for breaking them, too. If they have a say about rules and limits when it is appropriate, when the dishes are done, what hours are assigned for homework, how often the lawn is mowed, teenagers will be more agreeable about following rules you may have to lay down about serious issues like drugs, car privileges, curfew.

Reward good performance. According to the size and quality of a task, rewards can be simple, like a smile or praise, or sophisticated, like a trip to Hawaii. It is important to acknowledge or noticeably appreciate most positive performances, rather than emphasize poor work with criticism or punishment. Talk about standards for accomplishment and make it clear, through explanation and action, that excellence is achieved by progressive steps. Mistakes are necessary learning moments; by analyzing them, we can extract the information we need to improve the next step. A person's self-esteem is high when he can recognize a mistake or poor performance and not feel excessive guilt.

IX.
Power

In order to have high self-esteem, a person must have the *resources, opportunities* and *capability* to influence the circumstances of his or her own life. When a teenager experiences these qualities in his life, he will have a sense of Power. A sense of Power is expressed in his feelings and beliefs about his own capabilities. For example, he will:

- believe he can do what is required or what he decides to do at his age and position in life
- feel comfortable about assuming responsibility
- feel capable of making decisions and solving most of his problems
- feel that he can maintain control of himself, despite pressure or stress
- be able to use the skills he has in situations that require them
- think that he is becoming capable of taking charge of his own life

Power may be exercised in any of the following ways:

influencing people
making decisions
manipulating objects
controlling one's body
setting limits for oneself or others
demonstrating skill

taking responsibility
accomplishing purposes
controlling one's emotions
solving problems
learning
teaching

55

Resources that are critical to gaining a sense of Power are:

knowledge

health

physical capability

skills:

   manipulativeness

   decision-making

   problem-solving

   communication

material resources

tools

varied experiences

information available, beyond personal knowledge

Having a sense of Power is not the same as "being powerful." People or nations arm themselves when they feel insecure, not when they are confident about their own power. The teenager who excessively demonstrates "power" over others, physically or through psychological manipulation, is often making up for the lack of a sense of Power.

Power in Adolescence

The adolescent yearns to exert the power he feels in expanded knowledge, awareness, and social ability and in a maturing, or often fully adult, body.

He is no longer content to stay close to home, but wants to move around continually to be with friends, explore new places and opportunities. He may even feel perfectly capable of taking control of his own life, and want to move away from home before he is actually prepared to handle adult responsibilities. He will chafe more and more at the restrictions placed on his behavior by parents.

Example:

By the time she was a high school senior, Terri had a part-time job that enabled her to meet all personal expenses of recreation, clothes, and the many incidental fees and equipment she needed at school. She knew how to manage her time effectively and maintained good grades in school while performing responsibly at work. Her classmates listened to her opinions and respected her judgment. But at home, her parents still saw her as a young girl who needed constant protection and supervision. They required her to be home at 11 pm after dates and refused to listen to her reasons for a time extension after big school events. Her mother wanted to direct her choice of clothes. She was asked to account for all her time, whom she was with, and what they were doing. Terri wanted to be honest with her parents, but she saw their control as unreasonable for her age and felt they didn't trust her even though she was not doing "wrong" things. Her friends and teachers responded to her as a maturing young woman and she felt competent at school. But at home, she was frustrated and felt powerless. She began to tell little lies to get around her parents' restrictions, and investigate ways to leave home before graduation.

If an adolescent believes she has power over herself, parts of her life, and some situations, her self-esteem will be enhanced. Terri's self-esteem was still fairly high because she was demonstrating her competence every day to herself away from her parents. The communication problem between them required some outside help. Terri's grandmother had more trust in her good judgment than her parents did at the time. She and a school counselor gave the parents a broader perspective on adolescence in general and Terri's school performance in particular. Through discussion, they were able to reach compromises on rules, understand each others' points of view better, and clear up a potentially destructive situation. Terri's sense of Power and her self-esteem increased with this successful resolution.

When circumstances or attitudes within the family severely limit opportunities for the adolescent to exercise power in appropriate ways, he may seek other environments and relationships where he can assert himself. He may believe that he is perfectly capable of taking control of his own life, and want to move away from home before he has the *resources* and *capabilities* required to handle adult responsibilities. He will object more and more to the restrictions placed on his behavior by parents. Sometimes, during this period, teenagers make rebellious choices which can seriously restrict their life choices for years to come. Pregnancy, drug use and delinquency are the kinds of adolescent problems that may have consequences for some time.

Example:

Jan was not as fortunate as Terri in her conflict over power with her parents. Even as a little girl, Jan had a forceful personality which was encouraged and seldom limited by her permissive mother, who saw her strong will as "cute." Early divorce removed the father's discipline. Jan's mother encouraged freedom of expression and self-reliance. Jan was independent in her own desires and could take care of many of her own needs. By the time she entered high school, her body was already near maturity, and so were her ideas and interests. She wanted to associate with older teenagers and explore the same kinds of activities they did. At first, her early maturity seemed like a natural development of her strong personality. An occasional date with a high school senior couldn't be harmful. But as date requests became more frequent, night hours later, and Jan began to reject even her mother's minimal controls, the mother got scared.

During this same time the mother remarried, to a man whose ideas about child rearing were quite different from her own. He believed in firm rules, laid down by the parents, which were to be followed without question by children up to the age of eighteen. He was also concerned, rightfully, about Jan's dating and social habits. He decided to take the situation in hand by setting some clear limits on her behavior, such as 10 pm curfew, no dates with older boys, no more than 10 minutes on the phone, etc. The mother, frightened over the direction her daughter was taking, agreed with her new husband's proposals, despite the fact that they were a radical switch from any way she had ever handled Jan.

Jan's reaction to the new regime was predictable. She argued violently with her parents for a few days. When it was clear that they intended to hold firmly to the new rules and consequences, she devised numerous ways to outwit their system and go on doing what she wanted. She would be in by 10 pm, but crawl out the window after her parents were asleep; she would leave for school in the morning, but meet older friends, who were not in school, and spend the day hanging around the pool hall; she began to experiment with drugs with these friends.

Within a few weeks, reports of truancy came home from school. When the parents found out what was really happening in Jan's daily activities, the shock caused them to clamp down even harder. She was grounded completely. For two months she had to be home directly after school, no phone calls, no dates, etc. After a week of complete loss of a sense of power, with no say or choices of her own allowed, Jan acted desperately, in a way that would severely limit her life opportunities for many years to come. At sixteen, she couldn't possibly anticipate the consequences of her actions. One night she packed a small bag, crawled out of the window, and ran away. Her older friends helped keep her hidden away. Eventually, she hit the road, hitchhiking around the country with some of them. Within the year, she was pregnant.

At eighteen, Jan was facing the full responsibilities of adult life, including the care of her baby, but she did not have the resources, (no vocational skills, no high school diploma), the capabilities, (premature separation from family left her unprepared to care for a baby, manage money, or in any way assume a householder role), or the opportunities to gain a sense of Power over her circumstances. Instead, she was at the mercy of them. It would be a hard struggle, over a long time, before Jan could recover her early feelings of personal strength and regain her self-esteem.

Developing a Sense of Power: Problems and Solutions

The adolescent will gain a sense of Power when he has the opportunities, resources and capabilities to influence his own life in positive ways. When this sense of Power develops steadily and appropriately, self-esteem will be enhanced. But if the opportunity to exercise power is consistently denied, self-esteem will be lowered.

58

PROBLEMS WITH POWER

The teenager who isn't developing a secure sense of Power will behave in some of the following ways. He may:

- avoid taking responsibility. He will not initiate projects on his own and will have to be reminded about proscribed duties. He will shy away from challenging tasks.

- have limited skills in many areas. He may frequently respond to job requests with, "I don't know how," or "I could never do that."

- frequently act helpless or give up before a task is finished. He will avoid taking charge of others.

- lack emotional self-control. Most adolescents are subject to emotional outbursts some of the time. Chemical changes in their bodies bring about emotional ups and downs. But continual displays of anger, hysteria, fear, or an inability to deal with frustration, show a definite lack of personal control.

- be excessively demanding or stubborn.

- always want to be the leader or have his own way all the time. He will be inflexible and refuse to discuss or negotiate alternative ideas or activities, and refuse to share authority.

- avoid stating his own wishes and interests to others. Often he will follow whatever others say or want to do.

RELATING TO THE TEENAGER
WHO HAS AN INADEQUATE SENSE OF POWER

You can help your teenager gain a sense of Power if you will provide opportunities for him to exercise his own choices and assist him in developing the resources and capabilities he will need for adult life.

Encourage personal responsibility. When a teenager assumes responsibility for his own ideas and behavior, acknowledge it and show your appreciation. When he acts irresponsibly, confront him with the issue and appropriate consequences. Let an adolescent know he is responsible for what he feels. Explain and demonstrate how he can take charge of the way he reacts to people and events. Show him that he does not have to be a victim of other people's words, attitudes or actions. When he wants to blame others for his own difficulties, direct his awareness back to his own choices and possibilities in the situation. Support his own decisions, and hold him to them.

Help the teenager become aware of his own decision-making process. Talk through with him the steps he took to arrive at a decision. Ask him to consider alternatives that are available in any decision-making process, and help him think through the consequences over time.

Evaluate the problem-solving process. If you haven't done this before in the teenager's development, it's still not too late. Take him through the steps of solving a problem; show him different methods of approaching a problem, but let him take the lead in thinking through the alternatives and outcomes. Then give him lots of opportunities to solve his own problems and participate in solving family problems.

Affirm success. No matter how small, or in what area of life, build the teenager's confidence in himself by recognizing and appreciating his successes. Provide opportunities for him to practice and demonstrate things he can do particularly well.

Respect the teenager's present level of competence. He will still be in a learning and refining stage with many skills and will not be able to perform some tasks as well as you do. But it is important for you to appreciate what he can do at present, and praise him for it; this is the foundation for self-confidence.

Encourage the teenager to set personal goals, both short-term and long-term. Discuss with him (don't demand) what he expects and wants for himself. For example, ask what his goals are for the present school quarter or year. Ask what directions he would like to explore for life work. Your discussions should not be aimed at trying to persuade him to think or act towards objectives *you* have in mind, but rather to teach him the efficacy of planning ahead, according to specific goals.

Affirm him when the teenager influences others in a positive way. Point out, and demonstrate by example, effective ways of relating to others.

IMPROVING A SENSE OF POWER IN YOUR FAMILY OR GROUP

You can help all members of your family to build a sense of Power by providing many opportunities for each to exercise his own choices, responsibilities and authority.

Help teenagers refine their interpersonal skills. The family can provide an excellent practice arena for developing communication skills. Encourage members to voice their opinions and express their feelings, to listen attentively to others and honor each person's point of view. Your own example of respecting each member's say, and hearing him out before you interrupt, will be important.

Invite all members of the family to participate in making family rules and solving problems when appropriate. Practice democratic decision-making. Allow each member to air his feelings and opinions about problems or issues that affect the family—TV time, pet care, household and yard duties, assignments, etc. Whenever possible, don't alter family rules without first discussing them with everyone. Use majority vote and consensus when appropriate.

Communicate clearly about responsibilities and limits. See that each member understands what his duties are and be clear about the consequences for not performing them. Follow through with those consequences.[4] But allow the teenager to perform responsibilities in his own way, so that he can gain operational knowledge of his own talents. He may clean the house or do the laundry by a different formula from your own. But this is the way he tries out his own strengths and creativity. Ask teenagers to set limits for themselves and others. Be an example for this by setting firm and clear limits for yourself. Show, through your own behavior, how one can say "no" to unfair or unhealthy demands.

Set standards for achievements, but allow for mistakes. By example and explanation, ask for excellence in carrying out responsibilities and finishing projects. But also explain that excellence is achieved by progressive steps. Mistakes are necessary learning moments; by analyzing them, we can extract the information we need to improve the next step. A teenager's self-esteem is high when he can recognize a mistake or poor performance and not feel excessive guilt.

Utilize the personal resources of all family members. Wherever a teenager demonstrates a particular skill or interest, weave it into the fabric of your family life. Ask the creative teenager to help decorate the house for special occasions. Let a mechanically inclined son or daughter help you with plumbing or electrical maintenance. Ask your teenager to teach younger members of the family what he already knows. This will enhance his own skills, expanding his understanding for others, and promote Connectiveness within the family.

Accept teenagers' changes and evolution in roles. The son who was once your favorite game partner may be impatient with that role as he grows older. Respect his urge to let it go. The daughter who earlier took pride in accepting a mother role toward younger siblings may need to reject it completely in adolescence and move into the charming coquette role. These changes will require understanding and flexibility on your part, but they will also provide valuable practice for your own "letting go" process.

Spell out methods for handling grievances. Many nagging problems and conflicts within a family can be relieved when you set up a standard grievance procedure. You may allow each party in a disagreement or conflict to explain his position and complain completely, without interruption. Then act as the negotiator between the disagreeing parties in order to work out acceptable solutions. Or, all grievances can be aired at family meetings. If your policy is consistent, family members will come to trust their rights and opportunity for fair treatment.

Develop a balanced attitude about competition. The competitive spirit is fundamental to the western way of life and is usually a requirement for great accomplishment. It should not be thwarted in your family. But it will need to be refined so that one member's sense of competition doesn't become the damper, or the unmerciful goad, to another's achievement. Explain that it is not necessary to do best, or win, all the time. Teenagers will experience both successes and failures. They will feel better, and have a greater sense of Power, if their successes can somewhat outweigh their failures. You can assist them through attention, sharing your resources, and helping them turn mistakes and failures into later successes.

X.
Models

In order to have high self-esteem, an adolescent must have adequate human, philosophical and operational examples, or models, as reference points for developing meaningful values, goals, ideals, and personal standards.

Adequate human models help adolescents answer such questions as:

How should I be? A person like mother or father, or my favorite history teacher? Or is my older brother an example of how I would like to be?

How should I act? Do I know how to be a lady, mannerly and gracious? Do I want to act like that? Can I be strong in meeting difficulties and pressures like Dad does?

Whom do I respect? Who are the people I look up to most in my life? What qualities about them impress me? Which of these people influence me and how?

Whom can I look to for help? When I'm in a jam, who will be understanding and help me find solutions? Who can give me the information I need about this vocation, that school, etc.?

What is expected of me? Do my parents expect mediocre, or excellent, achievements from me? What standards must I meet at school for each of my teachers?

Adequate human models—parents, teachers, ministers, social and political leaders—can guide the adolescent in finding answers to many questions, some of which are not clearly asked. In the process, he will be able to start setting standards for himself and others, and learn how to solve problems and cope with new situations.

Adequate philosophical models help adolescents answer questions like:

What do I believe? Do I think democracy is the best form of government? Do I believe in God? Do I believe in capital punishment, premarital sex, etc.?

What is right? Is it right to always tell the truth? Is it o.k. to break a promise? Is it right to cut classes, smoke marijuana, cheat on an exam? Is it right for me to follow my parents' rules when I think they're unreasonable?

What is true? How can I tell? Can something be true for someone else, and not me? And vice-versa? Are my feelings true? Does the truth change?

Where am I going? Is a particular direction or purpose right for me? Should I go to college? What do I want by the time I'm twenty-five? What are my opportunities and capabilities?

What is important to me? Do I need love, and how can I get it? Do I want to achieve something big? Do I want money and fame? How much do I value my friends, my parents?

What is the meaning of things and what do I have faith in? Is there a meaningful order in this universe, or is it all just random happenings? Why is there suffering? Why are some people born deformed? Why do we die? Do I trust my parents to want the best for me? Do I have faith in my religion, and is it true? Do I have faith in mankind?

Philosophical models, provided by family philosophy, social mores, religion, or historical philosophies, will tend to merge and solidify the adolescent's mind. He can begin to develop a philosophical point of view which will lend personal security and guidance about goals and life choices.

Adequate operational models are mental constructs that help adolescents answer such questions as:

How do I do this thing? How do I put the pieces together so this problem, this machine, this project will work?

What standard must I meet? How many times do I need to do it, with what percentage of success? Shall I do my very best, or just get by?

What limit should I set? Can I drive over the speed limit here? How much of this shall I eat? How much can I spend on this date?

What will work? Will this camping plan see us through the whole trip? Can I take 7 classes this semester and only 3 next semester?

What rules should I follow? Shall I respect my parents' rules or go by the gang's? Can I make up my own rules now? Whose rules are really fair? Are the laws of our society the same for everyone? How far shall I follow them?

When the adolescent possesses adequate operational models, he will have skills that will make him secure in attempting new tasks. He will be productive and want to maintain excellence in performance.

One of the reasons that many adolescents do not learn effectively in school is that *they don't know how to go about learning.* Knowing how to go about learning requires a number of skills which some teenagers haven't learned well. Often the problem is not "psychological" or even "perceptual," but rather that the person has no firmly structured model for how to learn something. We need to teach people *how* to learn before they *can* learn, and many teenagers still do not have a concrete understanding of how they learn. Paying attention, overcoming distractions, handling stress, organizing material, etc., are all things that are learned.

Models in Adolescence

Heroes and ideals are very important to adolescents. They will "adopt" dramatic figures, movie or rock stars, explorers, inventors, athletes, etc., as models, and place them on a pedestal. They surround themselves with effects—posters, autographs, articles, records—of these heroes and try to imitate their dress or behavior. Or they choose impressive adults in their environment—a teacher, coach or big brother—as a hero to look up to. Even peers can become heroes—the class football star, brilliant debater or outrageous comic. Such heroes, which parents can usually assess with greater reality, may annoy parents and make them feel replaced. But hero worship at this stage is a way that adolescents search for Superhumanness, and standards to emulate.

Adults often find the adolescent obnoxiously idealistic. He may have dreams of solving the world food problem, or bringing people together in peace and brotherhood, or living an idyllic life off the land in some foreign paradise. He will be contemptuous of adults who "plod along" in a mundane life and announce that *he* never intends to waste his life with such insignificance. He may also become fanatically religious. Many "conversions" take place at this time of life. Through such extremes of views and visions the adolescent is exploring what he can believe in and what is really important to him.

Example:

Doug was a frightened, anxious thirteen year old with low self confidence. He didn't perform well in school and at home nothing he did was right. His alcoholic father berated him constantly and even though he was secretly ashamed of his father, he believed the complaints and accusations must be true. His mother, afraid of the father and under his control, never argued, and seemed to accept the father's appraisal of Doug. When he entered high school, Doug was small and hunched over in a hiding position. He was too timid to relate to classmates. But he liked swimming, so he forced himself to try out for the swimming team, even though he never expected acceptance. The swimming coach was tough and exacting, like Doug's father, but also fair, ready to carefully train talent, and supportive of his effort, unlike Doug's father. He put Doug on the lowest team and started training him harshly. Doug knew how to cope with harshness and keep going. The coach rewarded every show of progress, which made Doug work harder. Within a year, Doug had improved his swimming dramatically. He adopted the coach as his hero and began to imitate him in dress, haircut, physical manner, (straight and swaggering), and even speech. He was feeling much better about himself and looked forward to mounting successes with the swimming team.

During his four years at high school, Doug distinguished himself as a fine swimmer, winning many trophies and admiration from peers. His grades improved; he looked forward to applying for a college scholarship. His physical bearing had changed completely from that of a "weakling" to a strong, straight, tanned young man. He felt confident of his physical ability and had learned the discipline required to make progress at almost any task. In the years that followed, Doug gradually expanded his view of life and his aims beyond those of the coach and gave up his dependence on the man. But his teenage hero had provided a model for personal strength, discipline and achievement that saved Doug in a critical time.

Developing Human, Philosophical and Operational Models

Adolescents who have grown up with strong, responsible human models whom they could rely on and respect, who have been exposed to understandable and consistent guidelines for their behavior through philosophical models, and who have been taught, at home and in school, many different processes, and skills for coping with daily life via operational models, will have a healthy sense of Models. They will feel secure about order in their lives, and will usually be able to make sense out of what is happening. They will be able to determine right from wrong most of the time. Their values and beliefs will serve to consistently guide their behavior and goals; they will have a sense of purpose and direction. They will know how to learn and how to meet standards of excellence.

If sufficient models were not available as the child was growing up, you will need to fill them out during adolescence. His natural yearning for heroes, ideals and dreams will assist you in promoting a sense of Models for the teenager.

PROBLEMS WITH MODELS

An adolescent with an inadequate sense of Models will act in certain ways. He may:

- get confused easily. He will waste time with apparently aimless activity, or sometimes become obsessively involved with activity unrelated to the task at hand.

- be poorly organized, in thinking and behavior. He may be sloppy or disorganized with himself and materials. His room will be messy.

- be confused about right and wrong.

- have a difficult time deciding what to say or do.

- respond to instructions in a confused or rebellious way.

- be unsure about methods and aims when working with others. He will continually seek directions or insist there is only one way of doing things.

- have rigid standards and get upset when others don't conform to them.

- avoid, or act awkwardly in, social situations where formal etiquette is required.

RELATING TO THE TEENAGER
WHO HAS A LOW SENSE OF MODELS

You can assist your teenager in developing human, philosophical and operational models by providing additional exposure to exemplary people and philosophies, and becoming actively involved in teaching him skills and processes.

Remember that you are a primary model for your teenagers. Exemplify principles of right conduct in your own behavior. Be an example of acting according to your beliefs.

Expose teenagers to people you hold in high regard either through personal contact or in literature. Provide opportunities for them to associate with noteworthy teachers, ministers, community leaders, or relatives. Discuss great historical leaders.

Help adolescents understand what they believe. Talk about their values with them. Challenge them to think about what they believe. Share what you believe. Let them know where you stand on philosophical, religious and social issues. When they ask what you think, tell them honestly.

Help adolescents set realistic goals for their behavior, and their learning. Ask them to state specifically what they want to do, or believe is right to do. Question them about the steps required to meet goals. Sometimes offer suggestions for their improvement. Ask them to decide what, and how much, they can learn. Encourage them to do more at times, but be ready to accept the choices they make about learning.

Make teenagers face the consequences of their behavior. Be clear about the cause and effect relationship between how they act and what happens because of it. Tell them exactly what your own expectations for their behavior are, and then be consistent in following through with rewards and consequences.

Help adolescents gain a clear understanding of how to do tasks. Spend time teaching the "how" and "why" of jobs they have not yet learned. Give explicit directions and demonstrate them. Do not expect a teenager to do a job you are not able or willing to do.

Emphasize strengths, rather than handicaps and liabilities, in your adolescents. Acquaint them with people who have overcome obstacles and weaknesses to achieve what they wanted.

Make an effort to understand the special conditions—local and broader societal pressures—that influence your teenager's behavior. Find out how other teenagers think, dress and behave. Try to understand the hopes and fears that motivate them. Allow for these pressures in your discussions and activities with your teenager. *Understanding does not mean permissive acceptance of destructive behavior.* A generation of permissive parenting has brought about confusion between understanding the reason for, and allowing, anti-social acts. We know many of the reasons why young people have burned buildings, taken drugs, rejected authority. Our understanding can help us listen more intently to criticisms and work together to correct social ills. It should not lead us to excuse harmful acts to self or others. You can say: "I understand that many of your classmates smoke marijuana. I understand that social pressure is heavy on you to smoke with them. I have read many of the studies about its effects and I believe that I am well informed. I realize it's a hard strain for you in some circumstances to reject it, but here are the reasons why it will not be accepted in this family, etc." Talk through with your teenager such situations and actions where he can either hurt, or help, himself and others. Hear him out. Try to reach common decisions or rules through mutual discussion. When agreement is not possible, you still have the last say, but your reasoning and your regard for his point of view will strengthen a bond of respect between you.

IMPROVING A SENSE OF MODELS IN YOUR FAMILY

When you provide a reasonable sense of order and purpose within your family you will enhance every member's sense of Models.

Communicate rules, policies and standards fully and honestly to all family members. Let family members know what you expect of them in terms of behavior, productivity, relationships and personal attitudes and make standards of performance clear. Define limits for behavior and follow through with them consistently. Show by explanation and example what "quality" work is and affirm it every time it is achieved. Provide opportunities whenever possible for family members to help determine rules, policies and goals.

Make the family a practice ground for refining interpersonal skills. Talk about relationships in your family. Work through disagreements and conflicts between members as they develop, rather than letting them build up into hardened negative feelings. Plan and carry out activities together.

Emphasize order in the family environment and operations. Make your home, and yourself, attractive. Set up order-keeping tasks for each member of the family. Teach members how to maintain reasonable order while working, for example, while cooking, building things, or doing creative activities. Suggest ways adolescents may organize themselves, their rooms and possessions.

Attend enjoyable events with your family that broaden cultural understanding. Go to lectures, concerts and fairs together. Expose your family to a wide range of individual achievement.

Encourage family discussions of beliefs, values and interests. Ask all members to share what is important to them. Don't require that everyone think alike or hold the same beliefs. Allow your family to provide an open forum for the investigation and comparison of different values and belief systems.

Encourage knowledge of heroes, and heroic acts, that form positive models. Biographies of great people—from books, television or movies—can be discussed in the family. Tell about ancestors who triumphed over difficult odds. Try to see positive qualities in the heroes your teenager chooses.

71

XI.
Evaluating the Four Conditions of Self-Esteem in Your Family

In order to determine those conditions of self-esteem which require further growth in your family, you will first need to observe and evaluate adolescents with a fresh eye. In reading this manual, numerous thoughts and new views will already have occurred to you about your adolescent's self-esteem and behavior. You may want to add to these perceptions by taking a few days to observe behavior, and listen to what your teenager says, WITHOUT JUDGMENT, before you determine a program to improve self-esteem.

When you observe dispassionately, as the scientist watches subjects, you will probably become aware of many characteristics and behavior patterns in your adolescents that have previously slipped past you in the rush of usual routines. Try to notice nonverbal cues—facial expressions, general bodily posture and movements—your teenager expresses in many different situations. Watch how he handles objects and organizes tasks.

Above all, try to *listen actively* to your teenager. Hear him out without interrupting or arguing. Ask yourself if you have heard what he is saying well enough to repeat it. Be aware of his tone of voice and the kinds of words he chooses. And learn to listen from your heart to the feelings beneath what he is saying. The teenager who launches into a long tirade about his sister's misuse of his possessions—"She comes into my room and takes my stuff all the time without asking me. . . . She's selfish too, she won't even let me borrow her new bike. . . . She lost the book I was reading last week. . . ." may actually be expressing a sense of neglect. The real message underneath may go something like—"Why did she get a new bike and I didn't get anything? Do you care for her more than me?"

If you practice listening to get both the actual content and the feelings in the teenager's talk, without reacting until he is finished, you will probably learn new things about him. And you will find that when you start listening actively to him, your teenager will feel that you value him more.

A Note About Anxiety and Insecurity

Feelings of anxiety and insecurity are chief factors in causing inappropriate behavior. Kids who are energetic or aggressive often don't "look" as if they are anxious, but in observing them, you might see signs of anxiety. An adolescent will express anxiety through a variety of body movements. What you seek to find through observation is the degree to which anxiety is present, and the conditions which seem to promote it.

Anxiety is expressed in the following ways:

foot tapping	rocking while sitting or standing
leg swinging	touching body or clothing excessively
pulling at hair	placing fingers or objects in mouth
tension in body	playing with mouth, tongue, or teeth
quick, jerky movements	lack of variety in facial expressions

Making Sense of Observations

After you have observed, and actively listened to, your teenager for awhile, you can start putting together what you have learned with your understanding of the four conditions of self-esteem. The following are questions you may ask yourself to help determine where you can assist him:

- Does my teenager have a broad range of relationships that are satisfying to him? Does he take an active part in our family life? Does he have a few intimate friends or confidants? Can he communicate easily and spontaneously? (Connectiveness)

- Does my teenager seem to respect himself as a unique and valuable person? Does he express several special talents and qualities? Can he allow himself to be different and stand out from the crowd? (Uniqueness)

- Does my teenager display strength of will and purpose when relating to people and performing tasks? Can he stand up for himself? Is he confident in putting forth his own ideas, beliefs and ways of doing things? (Power)

- Does my teenager have worthwhile heroes and exemplary people he can look up to? Does he show through words and behavior that he has clear values, beliefs and standards of conduct? Does his conscience express itself in his behavior? Does he know how to do many things and feel confident in undertaking new projects? (Models)

- Finally, given what you have observed, put together with what you already know, what self-esteem condition(s) need enhancing?

XII.
Deciding on a Program to Enhance Self-Esteem

After you have determined the condition(s) that can be improved, you are ready to select the behaviors and activities related to that condition from this manual that can be *comfortably integrated* into your family routines and life style. Obviously it would be impossible, and unnecessary, to try all of the suggestions given. Choose those you know you can consistently carry out. *Even one suggestion from a condition, applied steadily over time, will have a positive effect.* And as one self-esteem-enhancing behavior becomes a habit with you, it will not only begin to show in your adolescent's improved self-esteem, but it will serve as an example to him for relating positively to other members of the family. After awhile, family members will be conditioned to help each other. After you have mastered one change, add another.

If several of your children are old enough, you may wish to initiate a self-esteem improving program through family agreement. Talk over the conditions within the family. Ask them directly how each member feels about his own sense of Connectiveness, Uniqueness, Power and Models. Discuss which condition(s) are causing problems and decide together what new behavior patterns could help improve them.

XIII.
Evaluating Your Own Relationship with Adolescents

Few contemporary parents get through their children's adolescence unscathed. While the teenager works through, in roller-coaster rhythm, his many growth stages, social pressures, moods, fads, rebellions and heart-breaks, the parents often feel they are barely hanging on. They feel anxiety over their teenager's welfare. They may even become angry over the incessant problems and disruptions in a life that was much smoother and more predictable when their children were younger. And then they feel guilty for having felt angry. Raising children, and particularly shepherding them through adolescence, is easily one of the most demanding and complicated jobs anyone can do. Parents need lots of compassion, too, while they are trying to be compassionate toward their teenagers.

It is easy enough to find out, in countless books and articles, how we *should* feel toward our adolescents. But how we *actually are* with them and feel toward them may be far from those ideal states. Adolescent development and problems may threaten us in many ways. If we learn to recognize the threat and deal with our feelings honestly, we can work through problems more effectively. When we face our inner feelings towards adolescents we can help them more.

Below are some questions you might ask yourself to help you evaluate honestly how you feel toward your teenager:

What do I actually feel toward my teenager at this time?

What do my teenagers mean to me?

How do I really view this stage?

In my own future, am I considering my teenagers as insurance against financial need, or loneliness?

Do I want to realize my own ambitions through them?

Do I distrust their judgments and actions because I was unreliable as an adolescent?

Do I feel burdened emotionally and financially by their needs?

Does their youth, vitality, and promise in life make me feel less able, or defeated in my own life?

Does my own feeling of urgency about the passage of time cause me to demand more of my teenager?

Do I see myself as a molder of my adolescent, or a nurturer?

Do I feel afraid of losing control and power over them?

These may be hard questions to face. But answering them honestly will open the way for you to accept yourself, and your teenager, as human. Knowing how you actually think and feel about your teenagers, can help you plan actions that will create mutual respect. And you can gain support from others—spouse, close friends, counselors—by sharing honestly.

When you can accept and respect yourself for your reactions and feelings, you will be able to accept and respect your teenager's reactions and feelings more easily, too. And if you can see yourself as a person first and a parent second, you will probably nurture your teenager more fully. This is the time when you need to fully prepare to release your adolescent. You can do that more easily when you accept and respect your own unique self.

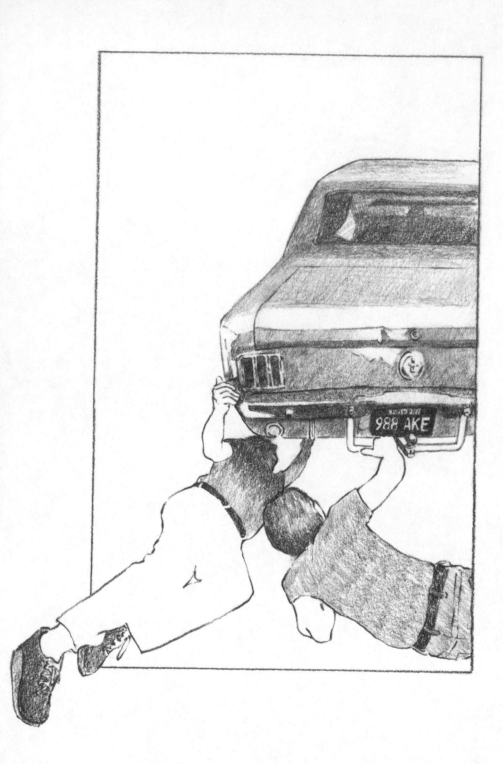

XIV.
Dealing with Your Negative Feelings

As you listen attentively to your teenager and try to understand his situation and point of view you may also feel what he feels—anger, frustration, disappointment, fear, etc. A certain amount of *empathy* from the heart is natural and shows you care for another person. But it won't help to get "bogged down" in his negative feelings. There is a difference between acknowledgement and acceptance of another's feelings, and *sympathy* to the point of taking on his fear, anger or despair in such a way that you are pulled down by it and consequently become an ineffectual helper. Remember that you can best help a person in emotional turmoil by staying separate from the turmoil and being clear-headed about the actual facts and possible solutions to the problem.

As you listen to your teenager's problem, be aware of the feeling overtones, and acknowledge them by reflecting back to him what you sense: "I understand that you are very upset about this event. . . . it's clear that you're really angry about the way she talked to you, etc." Calm acceptance of his feelings will let your teenager know that you are valuing him as a whole person, and not rejecting him for an emotional outburst. When you can acknowledge a feeling honestly, it will vent and spend itself before too long. Once the intensity of emotion has been expressed, your teenager will be able to move into a clearer state. With your guidance, he will be able to consider the issues of the situation in a more reasonable way. It isn't possible to be fair, logical and clear while you're in the emotional grip of a problem. You can save your teenager and yourself further frustration and time by allowing him to express the emotion fully before trying to evaluate the problem and seek solutions. With this method, you will also be teaching your teenager how to handle emotions within himself.

You also will be overcome by negative emotions sometimes. Contrary to the age-old myths of unconditional parental love that never flags, there will be times when you will literally feel hatred toward your teenager. Or you will be so angry you will feel like hitting him or her. When you face some of your own attitudes honestly, you may become overwhelmed with disappointment in yourself, and consequently guilt. All parents feel these ways sometimes. It will work best for you to face such feelings squarely, defining them to yourself or to another—your spouse, a friend, or counselor—in confidence. Some parents are afraid to admit these feelings, even to themselves, but they will tend to come out anyway, often in inappropriate ways. The parent who has a low-grade irritation toward his teenager over many unspoken and unresolved frustrations may have an over-violent outburst of anger at the teenager about a trivial matter: "Will you ever learn in your whole life to put the top on the toothpaste?" The parent who feels guilty about buried resentments may try to cover them over by indulging his teenager. "Here's $40, son. Take the car and have a good time.

It will go better for you and your teenager overall if you can admit your own feelings of anger, despair, guilt, even hatred, to yourself, and then start to deal with them honestly. Of course you will never want to say directly to your teenager, "I hate you!" although you might say "I hate what you're doing right now." But you can say, privately to yourself or in a journal, to a friend, or a counselor, "Sometimes I'm overcome with disgust toward this kid." Or, "I'm so mad at her that I feel like I never want to see her again." Later, after the heat of the emotion has cooled, such statements may seem ridiculous to you. But emotions aren't rational. They come about through a chemical reaction in your body. Negative emotions happen to everyone from time to time. The important thing for you to do is admit them at the moment. Admitting doesn't require acting upon. Accept them as you do your teenager's negative feelings. Say to yourself, "This is the way I feel right now." Later, when you're calm, you can think through the situation or the issues. Try to find the roots of your negative feeling and then consider what you can do to correct the situation. If Jennie's dirty socks in the bathroom day after day have finally evoked rage in you, you might want to consider if it's just the repetition of an inconsiderate habit, if you're also irritated with yourself for leaving things around and thus hesitate to correct her, or if you have simply failed to tell her in the first place that dirty socks are not acceptable on the floor but should be put in the clothes hamper.

When you have negative feelings, admit and accept them as normal and then go about rational problem solving. Don't add the negative feeling of guilt to your original negative feeling. If you have acted unfairly, yelled irrationally at your teenager, imposed a severe punishment, then apologize to him, forgive *yourself*, and let it go. Going over and over the scene out of a sense of guilt is useless; it will do nothing to repair whatever mistakes you might have made, nor will it move you toward solving the root problem. Be compassionate with yourself. Accept your own mistakes, as you accept your teenager's. When you do make a mistake, you can tell your teenager quite honestly that you recognize your unfair action as a mistake. He will then feel that you do have his best interests at heart. And he will enjoy a model for honesty and fairness, while observing an honorable way to handle mistakes.

If you find yourself feeling negative *most* of the time about your teenager, then you probably have a serious and long standing problem. If you keep falling into the same negative feeling cycle over and over, and can make no headway with either understanding or correcting it, then you would probably benefit from seeing a counselor with your teenager.

*   *   *   *   *

NOTE: We hope this handbook will assist you to improve the four conditions of self-esteem—Connectiveness, Uniqueness, Models, and Power—within your teenagers and yourself. Our suggestions for methods to enhance each of the four conditions given here are practical guidelines we have found workable with many parents and teenagers. As you reflect upon each of the conditions, remembering events and attitudes in your own life and within the lives of your teenagers, you will understand more specifically just how they work in *your* lives to promote, or detract from, self-esteem. Let your own creativity supply additional ways to enhance self-esteem. And enjoy the *whole* journey, from the first day's experiment, through an eventual family program.

—The Authors

NOTES

[1]For greater detail and assistance with self-esteem during this earlier stage, see Bean, R. and Clemes, *How to Raise Children's Self-Esteem*, Enrich, 1980.

[2]Purkey, W.W., *Self-Concept and School Achievement*, Prentice-Hall, 1970.

[3]Coopersmith, S., *The Antecedents of Self-Esteem*, W.H. Freeman, 1967.

[4]The whole realm of discipline and order within a family, including the need to clarify responsibilities, set limits and carry them out, is extremely important to healthy family life. These issues are addressed specifically in Bean, R. and Clemes, H., *How to Discipline Children Without Feeling Guilty*, Enrich, 1980.

NOTES

NOTES

NOTES

NOTES

NOTES

NOTES

NOTES